This Book Belongs To:

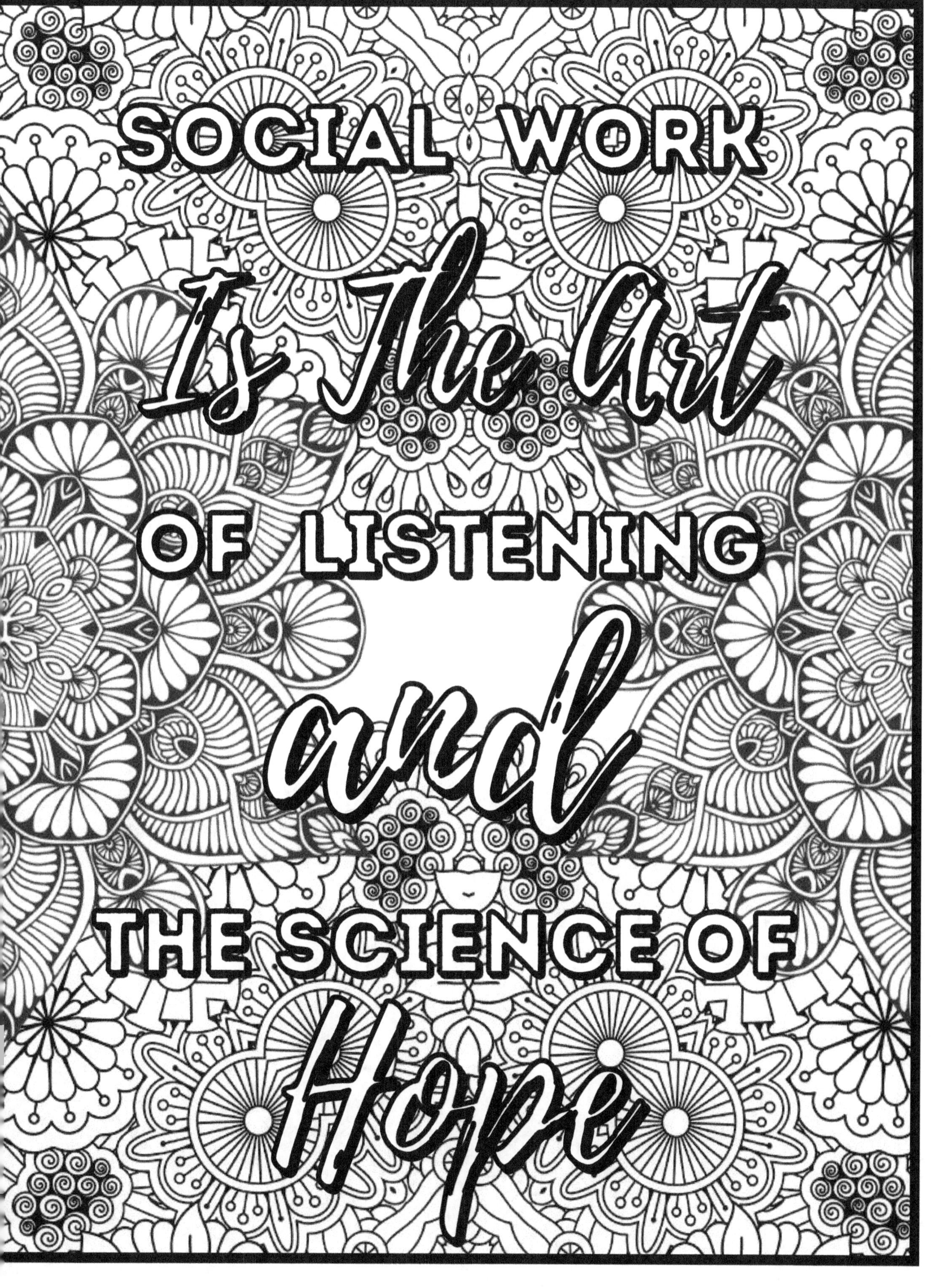

SOCIAL WORK
Is The Art
OF LISTENING
and
THE SCIENCE OF
Hope

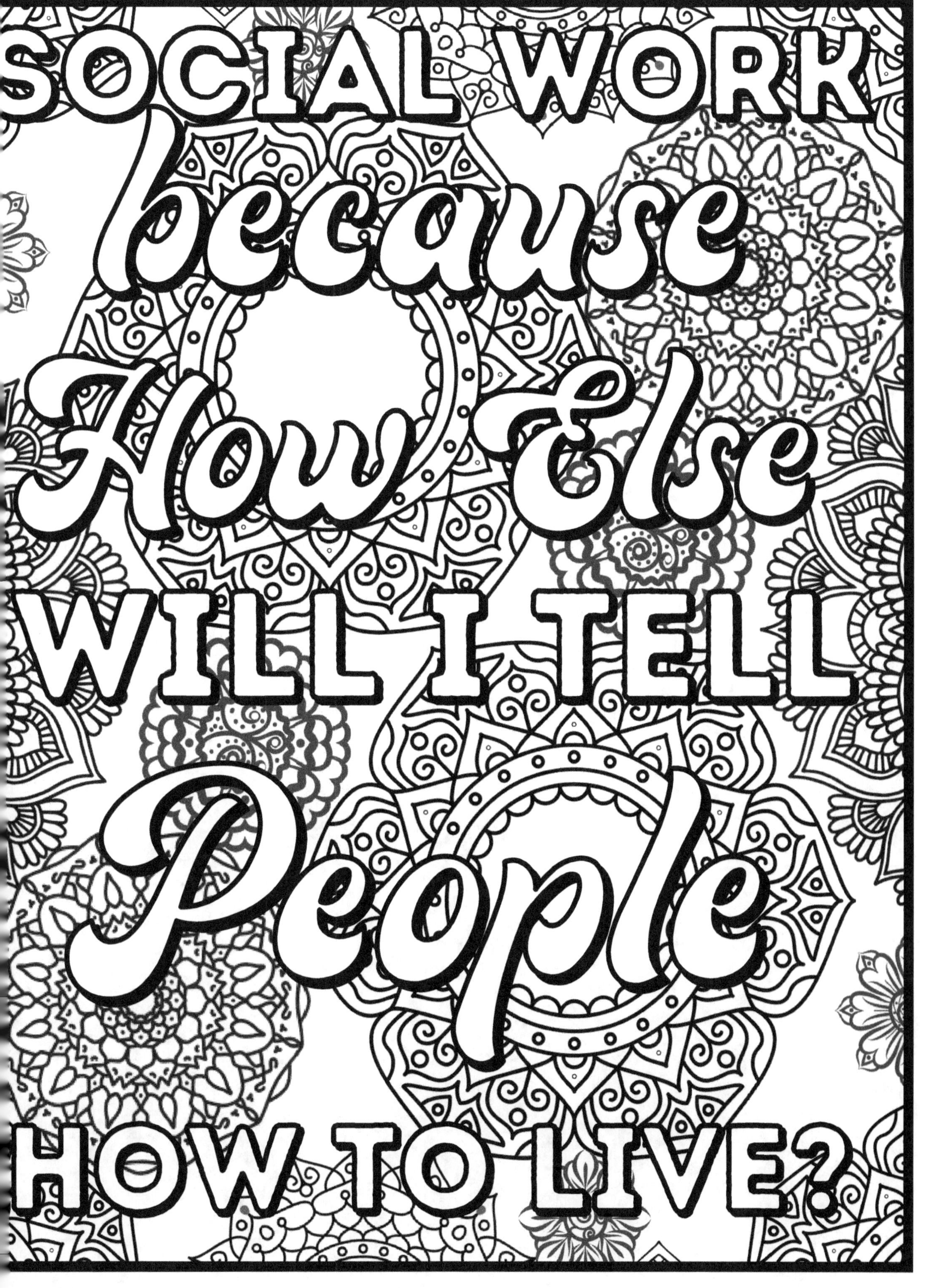

SOCIAL WORK
because
How Else
WILL I TELL
People
HOW TO LIVE?

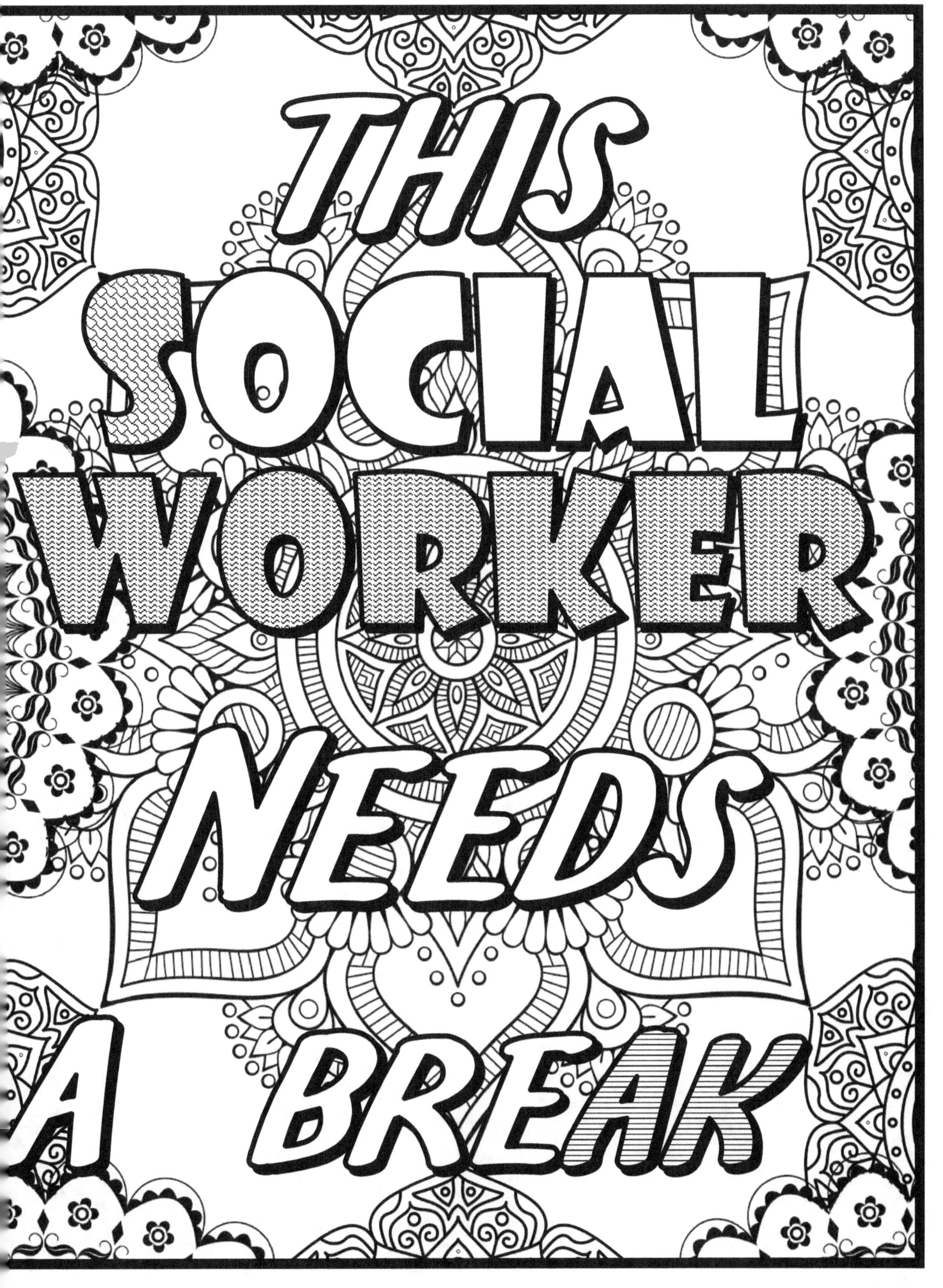

THIS
SOCIAL
WORKER
NEEDS
A BREAK

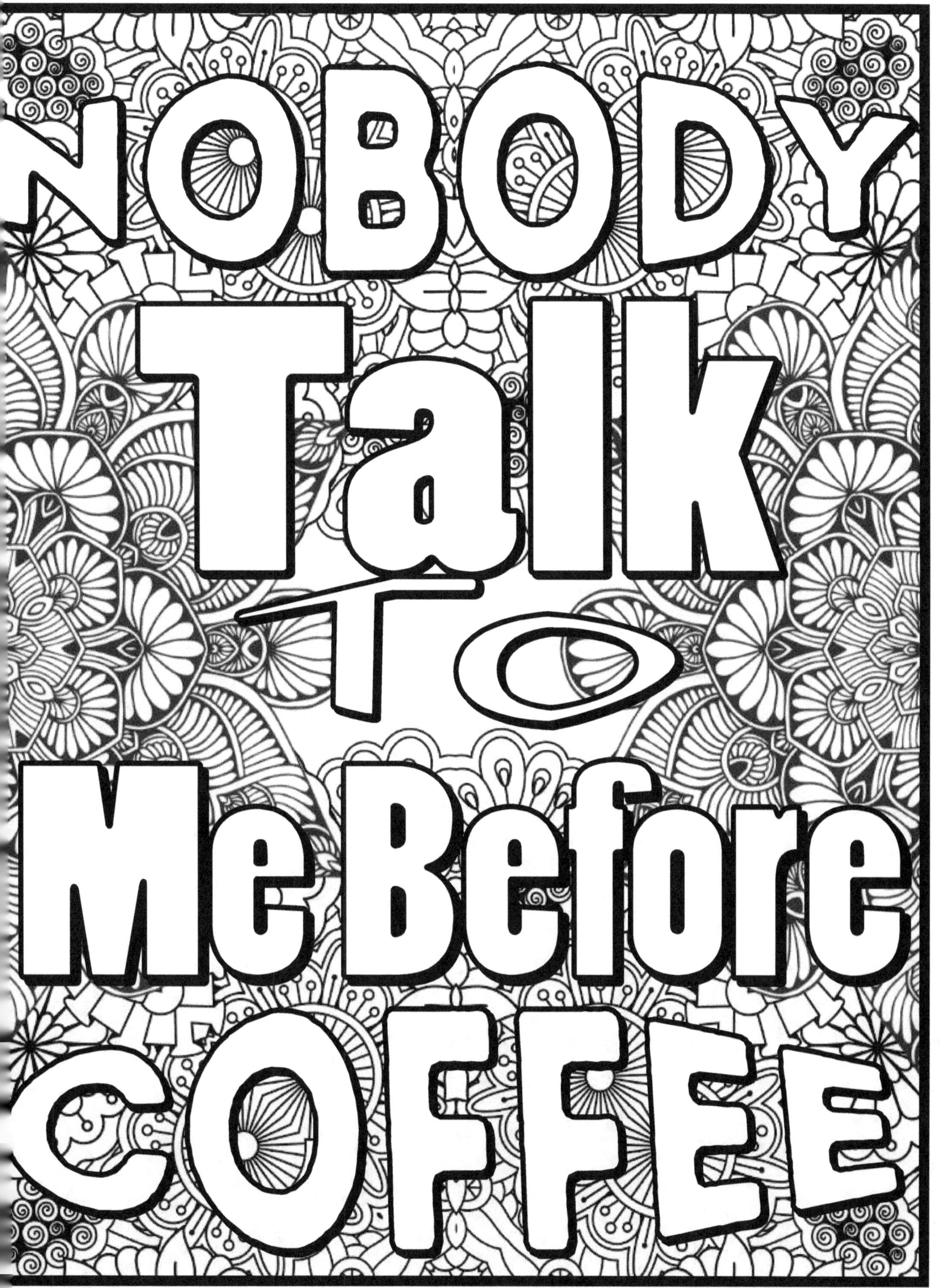

NOBODY
Talk to
Me Before
COFFEE

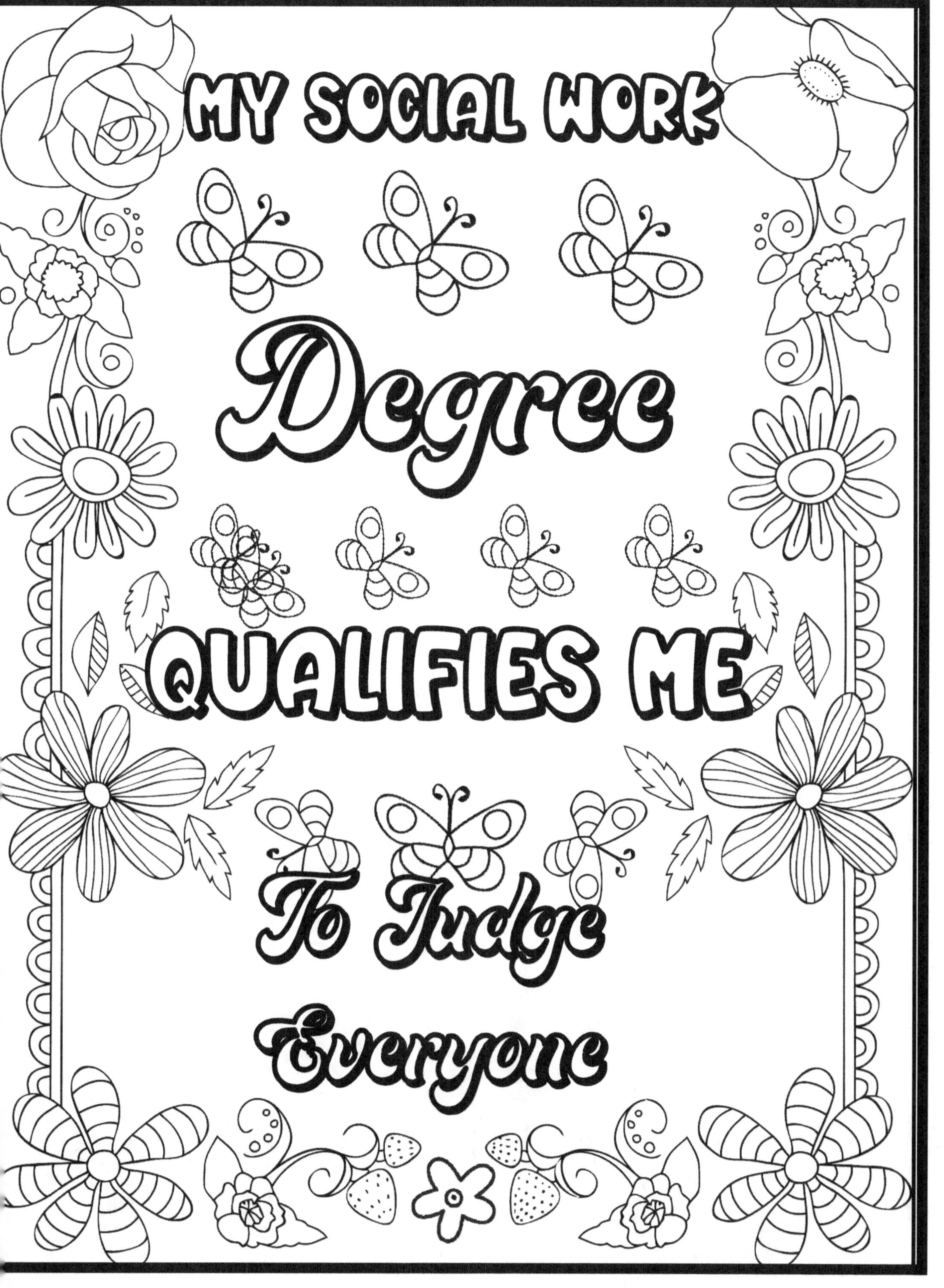

MY SOCIAL WORK
Degree
QUALIFIES ME
To Judge
Everyone

RELAX I'M
SOCIAL WORKER
I'VE SEEN
Worst

I BECAME
A SOCIAL
WORKER
for the Money
AND FAME

MASTERING
OTHERS
IS
STRENGTH

I AM A GOOD SOCIAL WORKER WHEN I'M NOT TIRED

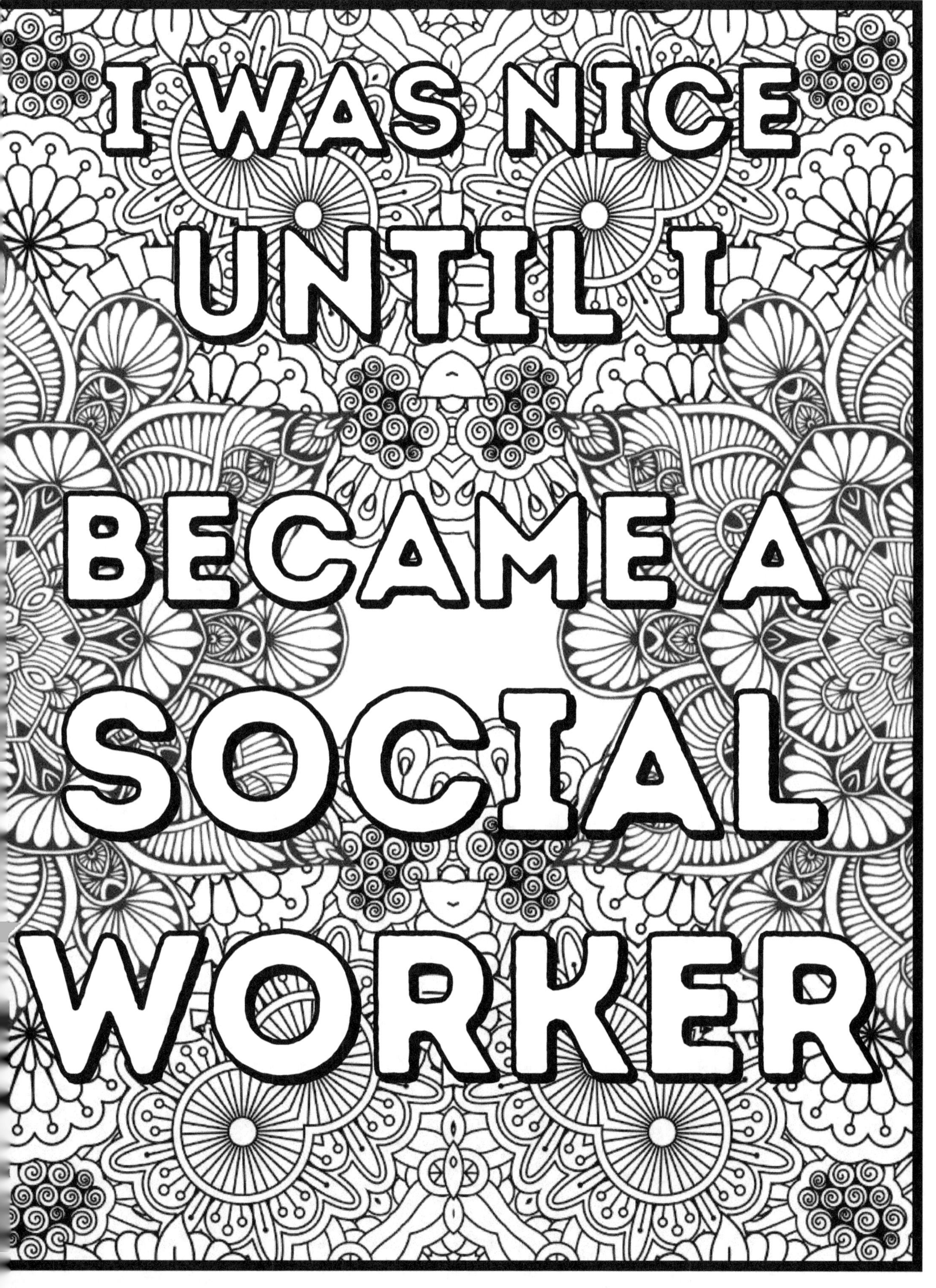

I WAS NICE
UNTIL I
BECAME A
SOCIAL
WORKER

KNOWING
YOURSELF
IS
TRUE WISDOM

SOCIAL
WORK IS MY
CARDIO

Miracle
Worker
During
9-5
Hours
Only

Trust Me
I'm
A
Social
Worker

Knowing
OTHERS
IS
INTELLIGENCE

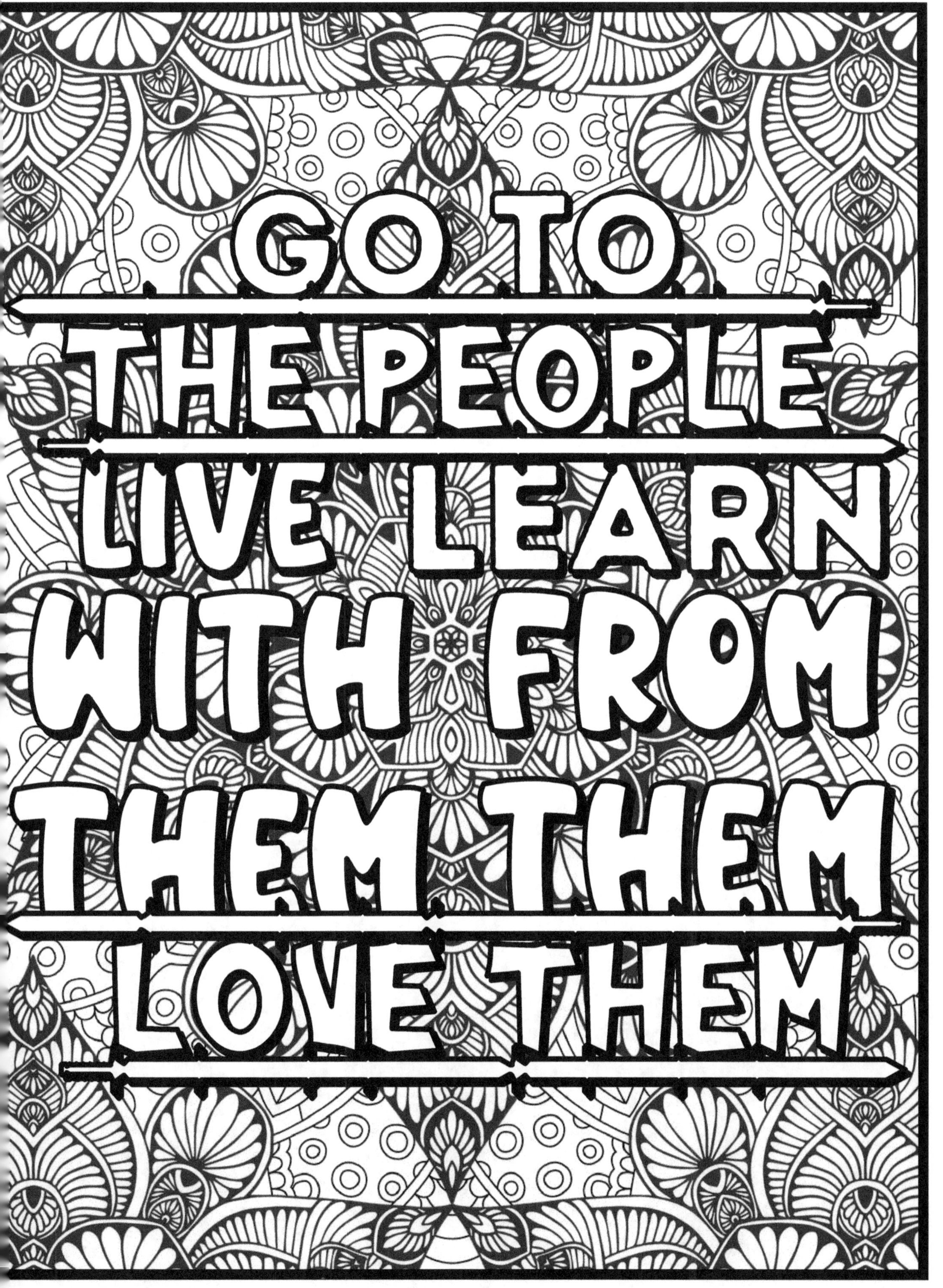

GO TO
THE PEOPLE
LIVE LEARN
WITH FROM
THEM THEM
LOVE THEM

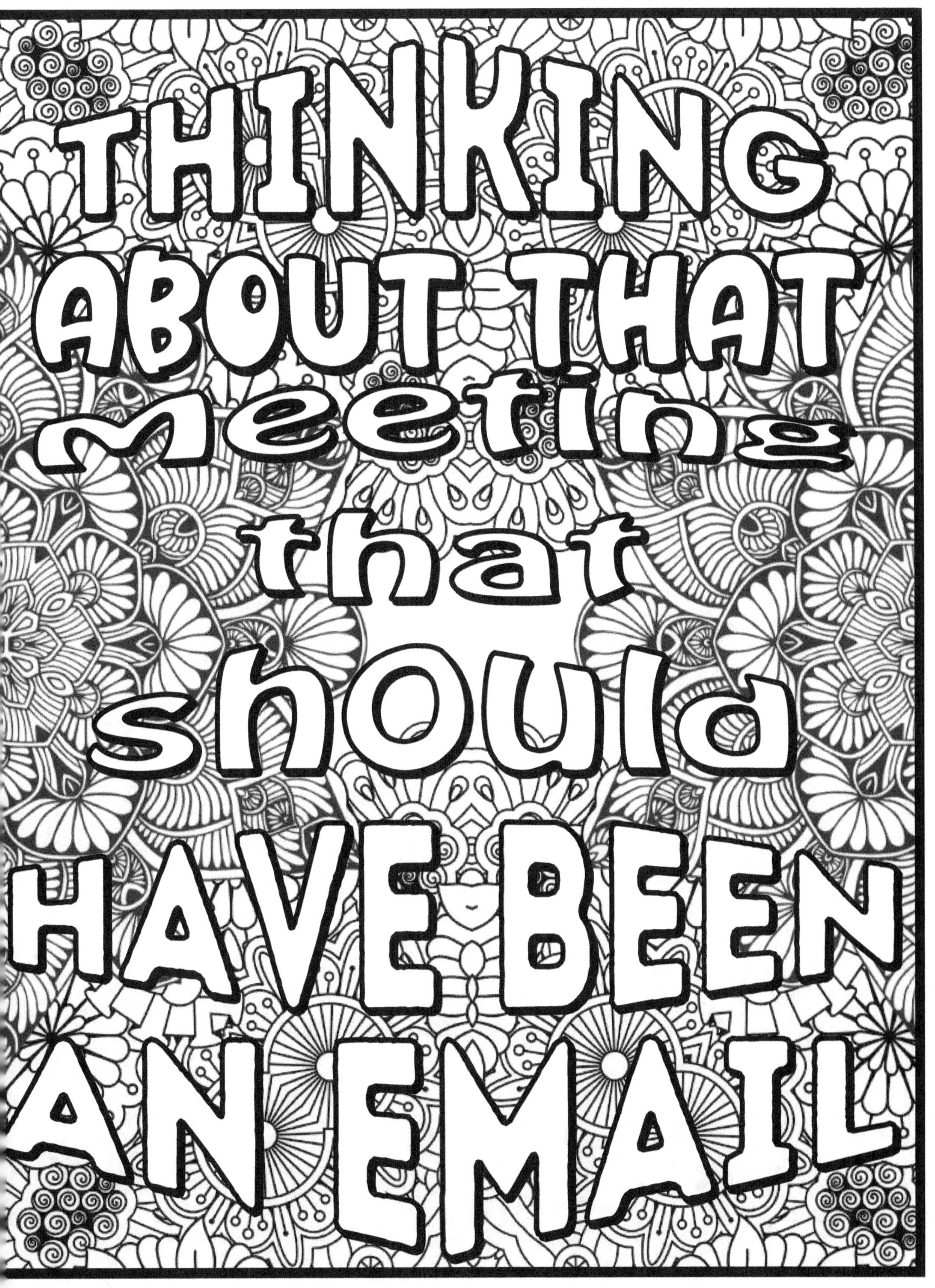

THINKING
ABOUT THAT
meeting
that
should
HAVE BEEN
AN EMAIL

THOSE WHO KNOW
DO NOT SPEAK
THOSE WHO SPEAK
DO NOT KNOW

MUSIC
IN THE SOUL
CAN BE HEARD
BY THE
UNIVERSE

As soon as you have made a Thought, laugh at it

TAKE CARE
WITH THE END
AS YOU DO
WITH THE
BEGINNING

RESPOND
intelligently
EVEN TO
unintelligent
TREATMENT

I Need To Take Off
Everyday
That Feels
Likes Monday

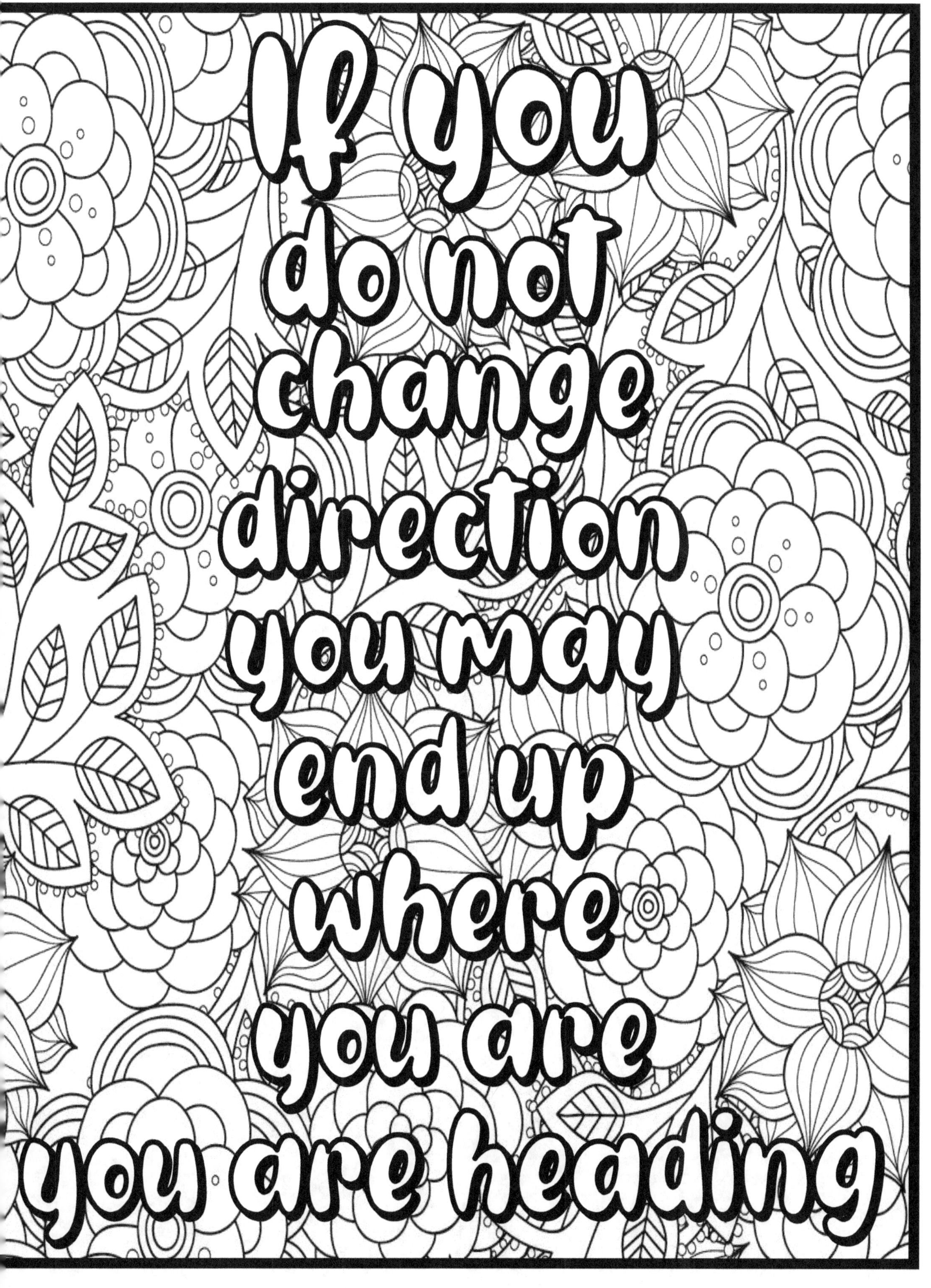

If you
do not
change
direction
you may
end up
where
you are
you are heading

To a
Mind that
is still
the whole
universe
surrenders

SINCERE WORDS ARE NOT FINE FINE WORDS ARE NOT SINCERE

THERE IS A TIME
TO LIVE
AND A TIME
TO DIE
BUT NEVER
TO REJECT
THE MOMENT

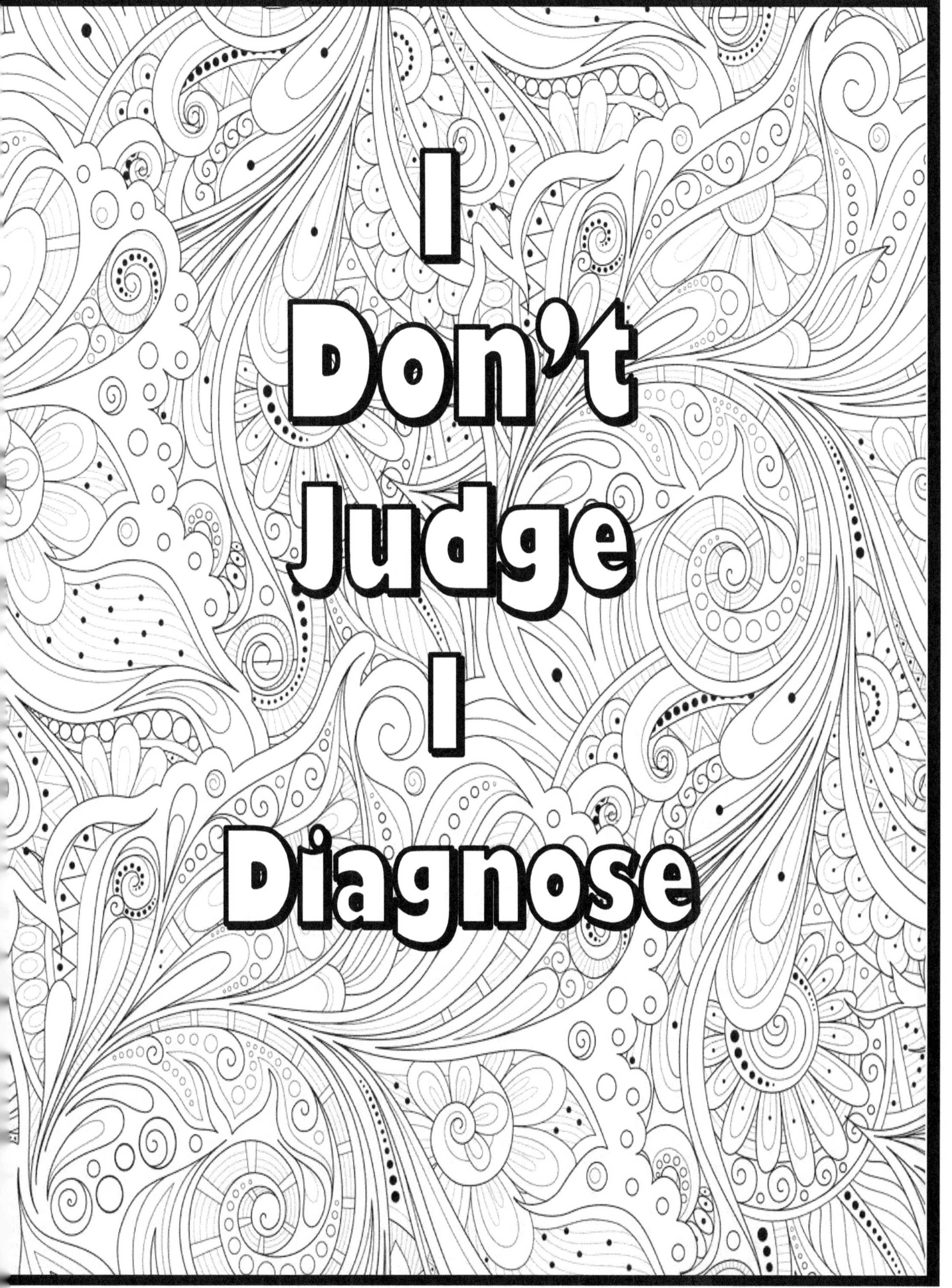

I
Don't
Judge
I
Diagnose

EVEN
MY PAPERWORK
HAS
PAPERWORK

i COPE
BY
LiSTENiNG
TO
TRAP
MUSiC

www.ingramcontent.com/pod-product-compliance
Lightning Source LLC
Chambersburg PA
CBHW081632250726
48657CB00009B/2843